39204000008553

D1504971

Sky Surfing

by Ellen Labrecque

Published by The Child's World®
1980 Lookout Drive
Mankato, MN 56003-1705
800-599-READ
www.childsworld.com

The Child's World®: Mary Berendes, Publishing Director
Shoreline Publishing Group, LLC: James Buckley Jr.,
    Production Director
The Design Lab: Design and production

ISBN 9781609732127
LCCN 2011940085

Photo credits: Cover: Corbis.
Interior: AP/Wide World: 15, 19, 27, 28; Corbis: 7, 16;
dreamstime.com: Ivica Peric 8, Vitaliy Afanasopulo
11, Speedfighter17 12, Adam Tinney 20; iStock: 24;
Courtesy Troy Hartman: 4, 23.

Printed in the United States of America

Table of Contents

Troy Hartman has a smile
on his face . . .
and a skysurfer
on his feet!

CHAPTER ONE

Surf's Way Up

Troy Hartman has a board strapped to his feet. Is he getting ready to snowboard down a mountain? No. Is he getting ready to ride an enormous wave? *No*.

He's getting ready to jump out of a plane 13,000 feet (3,962 meters) in the air! Hartman makes the leap. He stands straight up on the board. He does a flip, than a somersault, then he starts twisting around in a helicopter spin. He is doing all these tricks while **free falling** about 160 feet (49 meters) per second (109 miles per hour). Hartman is a world-class skysurfer!

Skysurfing is a sport that combines jumping out of a plane like a skydiver with aerial tricks, like those done by extreme snowboarders or surfers. When a skysurfer leaps from the plane, he stands up on a board. As he falls, he does twists and tricks. A skysurfer's feet are attached to the board, but the board can easily be removed if the skydiver needs to ditch it in mid-air.

In the early 1980s, a group of Southern California skydivers tried jumping out of planes while holding onto boogie boards. They laid flat on the boards and held onto the handles. They called this "air surfing." In 1987, French skydiver Joel Cruciani was the first to make the jump while standing in a surfing position. He used a regular-sized surfboard rigged with snowboard **bindings** for the feet.

The first skysurfers just used a regular surfboard.

What's a Wuffo?

Skysurfers are a brave bunch of people. They also sometimes tease people who aren't as brave. They even have a name for people who *won't* jump out of airplanes: They call non-jumpers wuffos! The word wuffo is a shortened version of "what for?" A non-jumper would ask: "Why would I jump out of an airplane? What for?"

This skydiver is not a "wuffo"!

By the 1990s, skysurfing was becoming more well known. Skydivers looking to **venture** out decided to give the sport a try. Competitive team skysurfing was included in ESPN's X Games from 1995 to 2000. Each team was made up of a freestyle performer, who did the tricks and stunts, and a cameraflyer, who used a helmet-mounted camera to film his partner. A panel of judges then watched the video. The winning teams were picked based on the tricks and the camera work.

In the 1990s, skysurfers also began to appear in commercials made by companies like Pepsi and AT&T. The Pepsi commercial featured Troy Hartman sharing his soda with a goose while skysurfing!

Let's take off and read more about this sport. The sky is the only limit!

CHAPTER TWO

Ready, Set, Jump!

A baby has to learn to crawl before he can walk. And, a daredevil must learn to *skydive* before he can *skysurf*. Skydiving is when a person jumps from an airplane. After they jump, they freefall through the air. After about three minutes, the jumper opens a parachute and comes to a soft landing.

About 350,000 people skydive per year. They combine for over three million jumps. There are also over 250 skydiving centers in the United States. These centers teach beginners how to skydive safely. They teach how to freefall, how to use skydiving equipment, and how to open and control the parachute. All these skills are must-knows for skysurfers as well.

Skysurfers must first learn the basics of skydiving.

Skydiving together is the easiest way to teach beginners.

Beginners can learn sky-diving by jumping **tandem**. This means they are attached to their instructor by a harness for the entire jump. They exit the plane together, jump together, and open up one parachute to land together. Many skydiving schools also use **wind tunnels** to teach their students. Wind tunnels create the feel of skydiving, without being thousands of feet above the earth.

Once a person has mastered skydiving, he can move on to skysurfing. Skysurfing is *really* tricky to learn. Many of the skydiving centers require students to have jumped out of an airplane at least 100 times before even attempting to skysurf.

Skysurfers need lots of training. They need to learn how to jump out of a plane with a board attached to their feet. Once in the air, they have to learn how to stand up on their board. (The wind wants to turn the person upside down). And eventually they have to learn to do tricks. They must also learn to position their body, and use the wind to help them with the twists and turns.

When his sleigh's out of order, does Santa switch to skysurfing?

The force of the wind on a skysurfer can actually make his skin ripple.

Skysurfers "surf" on boards called skyboards. Skyboards are like snowboards. Some skyboards are made of aluminum and graphite. Others are made of foam wrapped with fiberglass. These boards have foot bindings that keep the feet attached to the board.

Beginning skysurfers are trained with small skyboards because they are easier to control during freefall. They are about 35 inches long (88.9 centimeters) and weigh 2 pounds (.91 kilograms). The bigger skyboards, for more experienced jumpers, can be as long as 56 inches (142.2 centimeters) and weigh 2.6 pounds (1.2 kilograms).

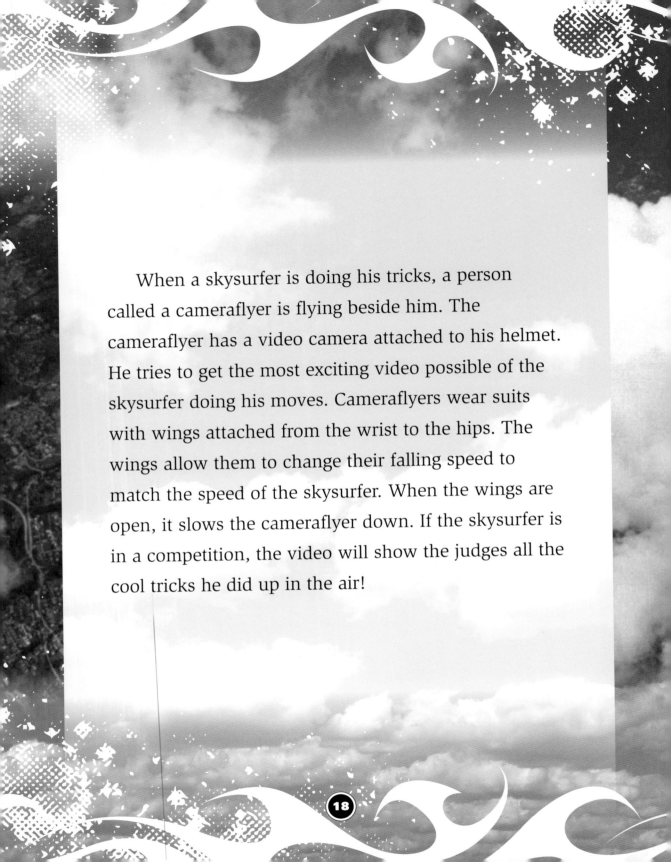

When a skysurfer is doing his tricks, a person called a cameraflyer is flying beside him. The cameraflyer has a video camera attached to his helmet. He tries to get the most exciting video possible of the skysurfer doing his moves. Cameraflyers wear suits with wings attached from the wrist to the hips. The wings allow them to change their falling speed to match the speed of the skysurfer. When the wings are open, it slows the cameraflyer down. If the skysurfer is in a competition, the video will show the judges all the cool tricks he did up in the air!

A cameraflyer and a skysurfer form a team high above the ground.

Many Air Force cadets become expert skydivers and perform in shows, as shown here.

CHAPTER THREE

Sky Stars

Want to learn how to skysurf? You can learn all you need to know from watching Troy Hartman! Troy is the best skysurfer in the world. Troy first learned how to parachute jump as a **cadet** at the U.S. Air Force Academy in Colorado Springs, Colorado. Later while living in Phoenix, Arizona, he started skysurfing.

Soon, Troy was skysurfing in movies and commercials. He also won a gold medal at ESPN's X Games. He was also the star of his own television show on MTV from 1999 to 2001 called *Senseless Acts of Videos*. In the show, Troy performed all kinds of crazy stunts. In one, he set his parachute on fire during a jump. In others, he crashed through glass windows. Despite doing these stunts, skysurfing is still his first true love.

"I can't get enough," Troy says about the sport. "It is a feeling like nothing else in the world."

If Troy is the best skysurfer in the world, then Joe Jennings is definitely the best cameraflyer out there as well. Joe has done more than 6,000 skydives with a camera mounted to his helmet!

"When I am up there shooting, I try to think a move or even two moves ahead of the skysurfer," says Joe. "I try to be way ahead of the game."

Jennings' most spectacular work came when he shot Troy for an **IMAX** skysurfing movie. It makes the viewers feel like they are in the movie too. When Troy shot for this type of film, he had to wear an 85-pound (38.6 kilograms) camera on his chest. He said the results make it all worth it.

"The thousands of people who watch the movie feel like they are flying too," he says.

Hartman and Jennings have created some of
the most amazing skysurfing videos together.

The flaps on a wingsuit help skydivers steer as they fall through the air.

Jennings has also filmed skysurfers doing other extreme sports in the air, such as wingsuit flying. A wingsuit is a jumpsuit with three huge wings sewn onto it. Two of the wings stretch from the wrist to the hip and armpits on each side of the body. The third wing is stretched between the jumper's legs. Each of the wings is made of parachute material that has cells that fill up with air. While in freefall, the wind fills the cells and the wings become firm like a raft. Now while falling, the person is also able to fly across the sky!

Finally, meet the best female skysurfer in the world (or should we say, "above the world"?).

Viviane Wegrath of Switzerland rocks on a sky-board. She has competed in skysurfing competitions around the world. She won two medals at the X Games. She also says that she feels more at home in the air than on the ground.

Next up: She plans to skysurf over the Andes Mountain in Chile. When she lands, she will drop her parachute and snowboard down a volcanic peak that rises 9,325 feet (2,842 m) in the air.

That's Viviane Wegrath on the right, taking part in X Games action.

When you're surfing down, it doesn't matter if you're down or up . . . until it's time to pull the 'chute!

Today, most skydiving centers don't allow anybody to try a jump—in a wingsuit, on a board, or with a parachute—until they are at least 18 years old. So for now, the best way to enjoy skysurfing and other extreme air sports is by watching all the great videos, staying in shape, and reading about the sport as much as you can. When the time comes, you'll be ready to experience some of the most exciting sports on earth and in the air!

Glossary

bindings—a device on a board, usually made of metal, that secures the feet to the board

cadet—a student in a military academy

free fall—the time after a jumper is out of the plane, but before he opens his parachute

IMAX—a type of movie shown on a very tall, wide, slightly curved screen

tandem—when one jumps while attached to another

venture—to take on a risky or dangerous task

wind tunnel—a tube that has a steady flow of air moving through it

BOOKS

Sky Diving
John E. Schindler (Gareth Stevens, 2005)
Covers the basics of skydiving.

Skysurfing
By Holly Cefrey (Rosen Books World, 2003)
A great introduction to skysurfing.

WEB SITES

For links to learn more about extreme sports: **childsworld.com/links**

Note to Parents, Teachers, and Librarians: We routinely verify our Web links to make sure they are safe and active sites. So encourage your readers to check them out!

Index

About the Author

Ellen Labrecque is a freelance writer who lives in Pennsylvania with her husband and two kids. She loves writing, running, and covering extreme sports.